Working as a Team

by Linda Kita-Bradley

Grass Roots Press

Working as a Team
© 2018 Grass Roots Press
www.grassrootsbooks.net

Acknowledgements

Grass Roots Press acknowledges the financial support of the Government of Canada for our publishing activities.

Canadä

Produced with the assistance of the Government of Alberta through the Alberta Multimedia Development Fund.

Alberta

Editor: Dr. Pat Campbell
Photography: Susan Rogers
Book design: Lara Minja, Lime Design Inc.

Library and Archives Canada Cataloguing in Publication

Kita-Bradley, Linda, 1958–, author
    Working as a team / Linda Kita-Bradley.

(Soft skills at work)
ISBN 978–1–77153–223–5 (softcover)

    1. Readers for new literates. 2. Readers—Teams in the workplace. I. Title.

PE1126.N43K5894 2018   428.6'2   C2017–906937–3

Printed in Canada

Part 1

Barb and Sam work at a gas station.

They work at the front counter.

They fill the candy shelf.

They make the coffee.

And they clean.

Barb and Sam don't like to clean.

And they don't like each other.

Barb is bossy.
Sam is not one to take orders.

"Here's the mop.
Clean the restroom."

Sam says, "You clean it."

Barb says, "Clean the coffee bar."

Sam says, "You clean it."

Barb says, "Take out the garbage!"

Sam walks away.

The restroom is dirty.

The coffee bar is messy.

The garbage is full.

The boss is mad.

The boss says, "Clean up this place!"

Sam mops the floor.
He is mad.

Barb takes out the garbage.
She is mad.

The boss is mad, too.

Talking About the Story

1. Imagine you work with Barb. She is bossy. What do you do or say?

2. What can Barb and Sam do to work as a team?

3. Do you know someone who is a good team player?

    What makes them a good team player?

Part 2

Read the next story
about Barb and Sam.

How is it different
from the first story?

Barb and Sam work at a gas station.

They work at the front counter.

They fill the candy shelf.

They make the coffee.

And they clean.

Barb and Sam don't like to clean.

And they don't like each other.

So, the gas station is always a mess.

One day, the boss gets mad.

"Clean up this place …

… or else!"

Barb and Sam clean up
the gas station.

Barb worries.
The boss is so mad!

Sam worries.
The boss is so mad!

Barb and Sam talk.

They make a list of cleaning jobs.

CLEANING PLAN

	MON	TUES	WED	TH
RESTROOM	SAM	BARB	SAM	BAR
MOP FLOOR	BARB	SAM	BARB	SA
GARBAGE	SAM	BARB	SAM	BAR
SWEEP FLOOR	BARB	SAM	BARB	SAM
COFFEE BAR	BARB	SAM	BARB	SAM
WIPE COUNTERS	SAM	BARB	SAM	BARE
TIDY SHELVES	BARB	SAM	BARB	SAM

They make a cleaning plan.

They hang the plan on the wall.

Barb and Sam are happy
with the plan.

Now, Barb and Sam work
as a team.

And the boss?
She is very happy.